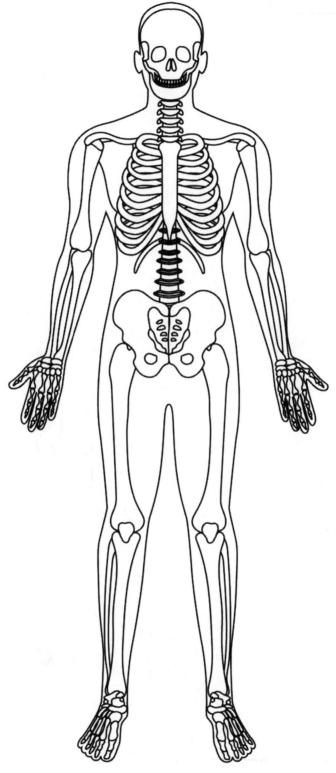

Skeletal System

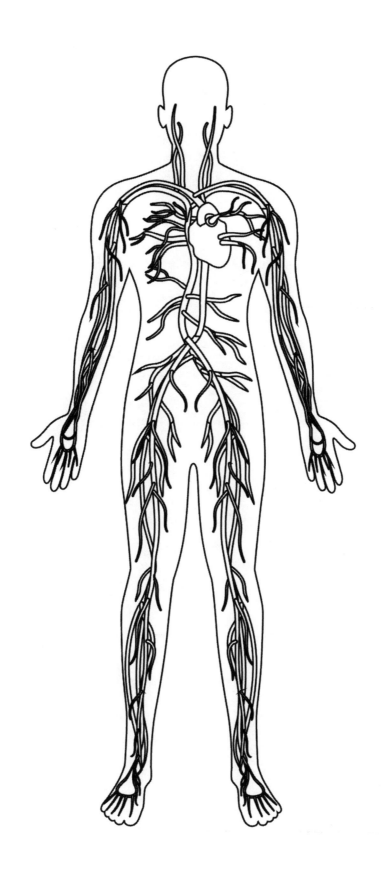

Circulatory System

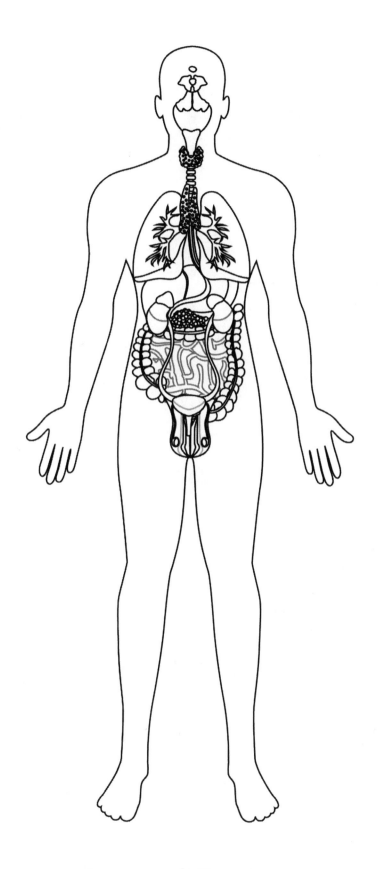

Internal Organs

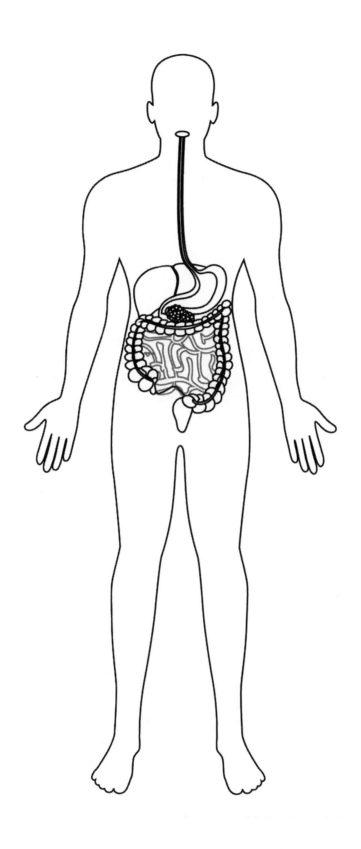

Digestive System

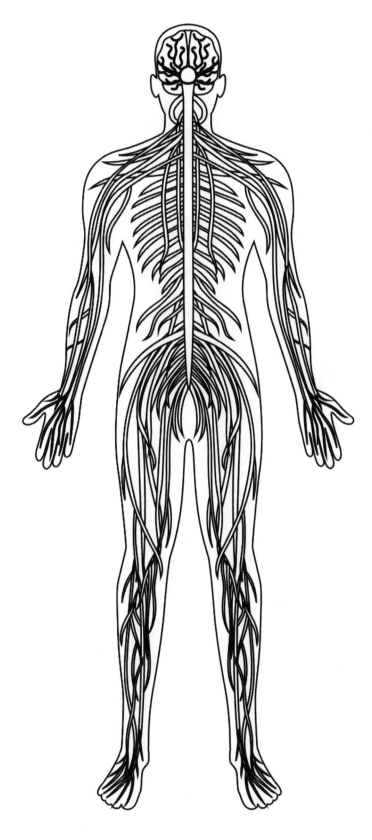

Nervous System

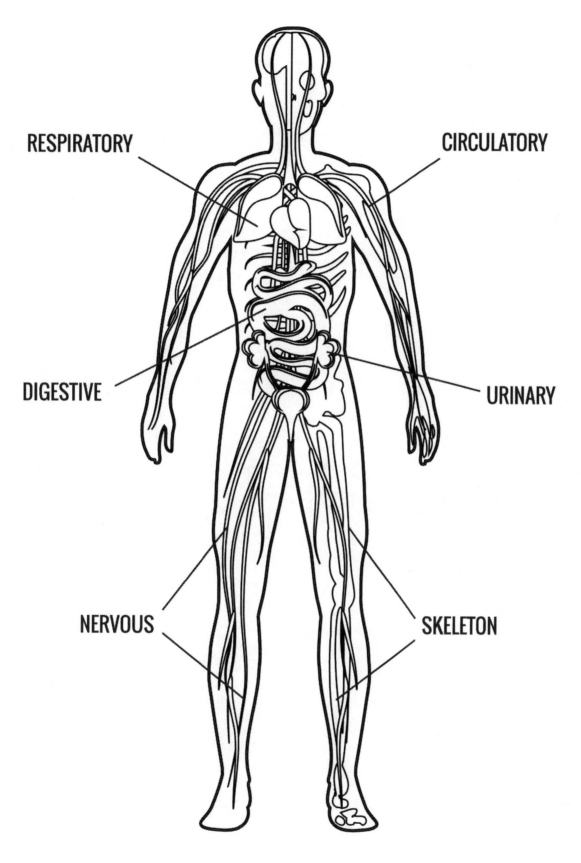

RESPIRATORY

CIRCULATORY

DIGESTIVE

URINARY

NERVOUS

SKELETON

Human Anatomy

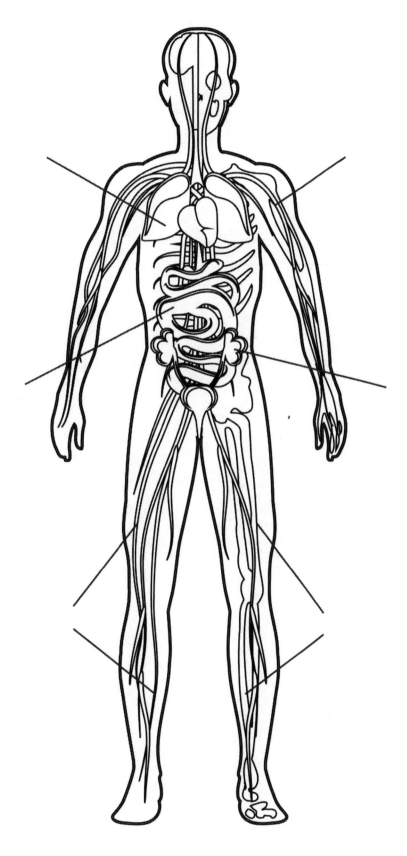

Human Anatomy

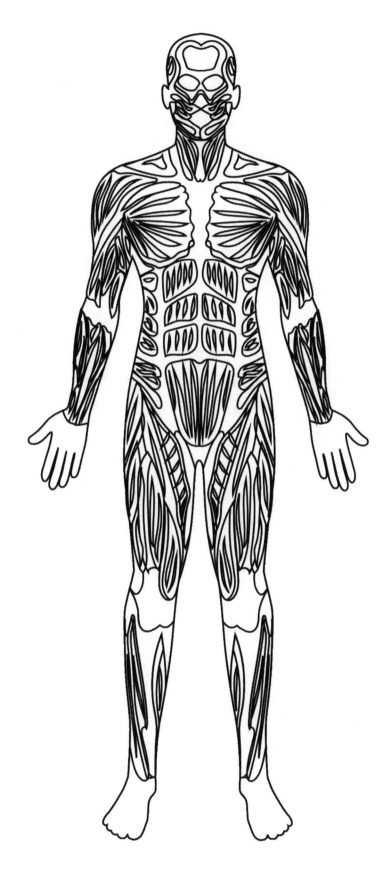

Muscular System

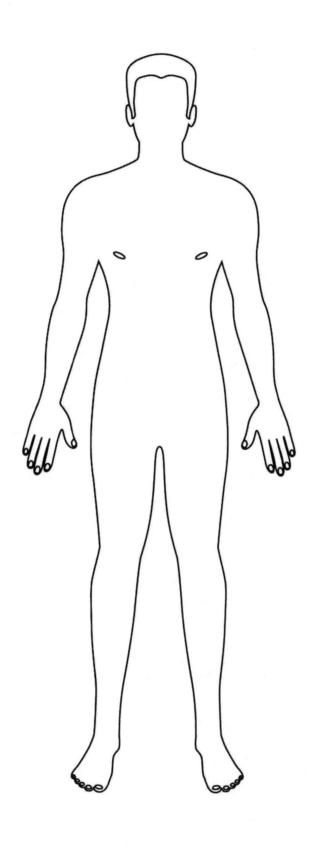

Integumentary System

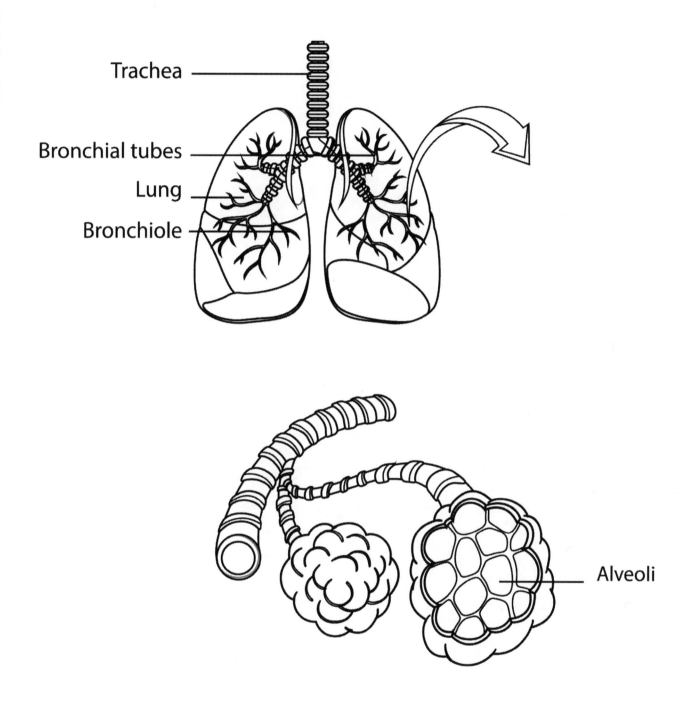

Trachea

Bronchial tubes

Lung

Bronchiole

Alveoli

Healthy Bronchiole and Alveoli

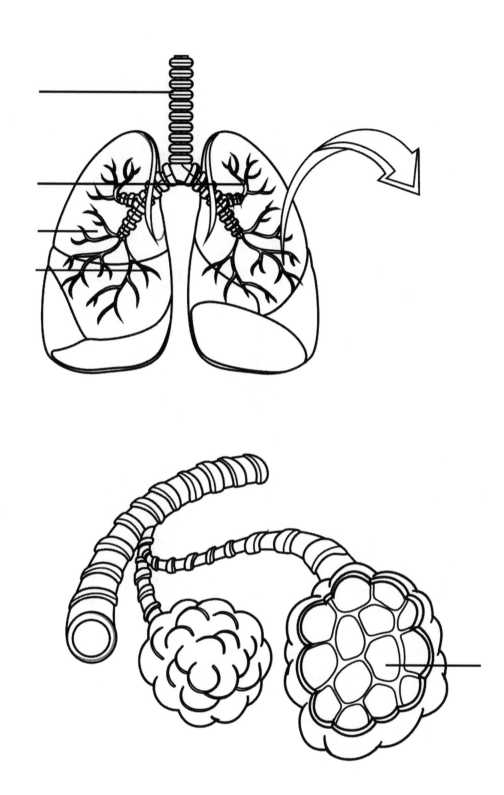

Healthy Bronchiole and Alveoli

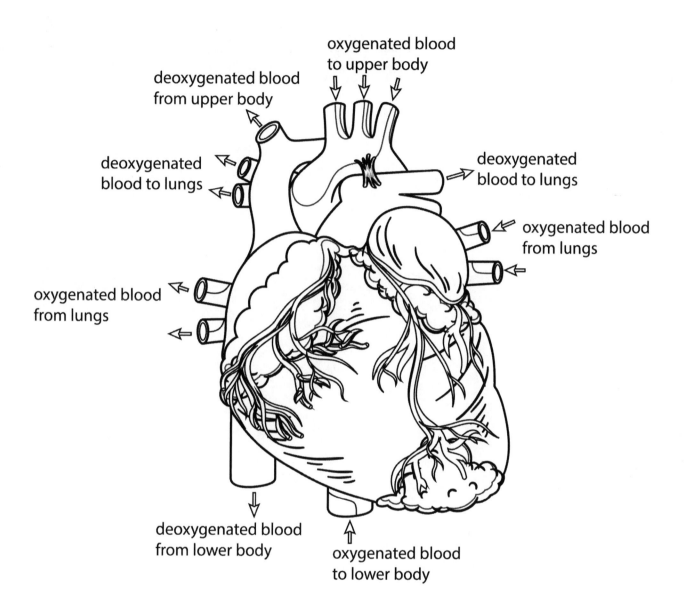

oxygenated blood
to upper body

deoxygenated blood
from upper body

deoxygenated
blood to lungs

deoxygenated
blood to lungs

oxygenated blood
from lungs

oxygenated blood
from lungs

deoxygenated blood
from lower body

oxygenated blood
to lower body

Blood Flow of the Human Heart

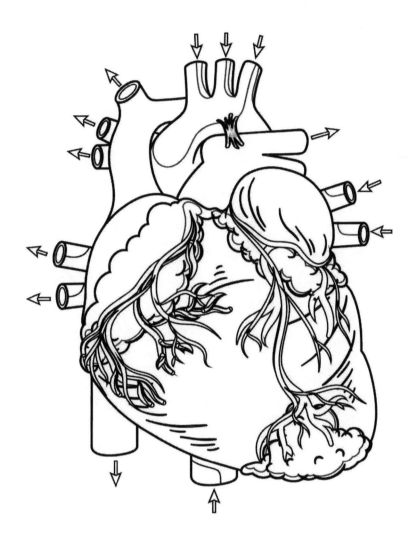

Blood Flow of the Human Heart

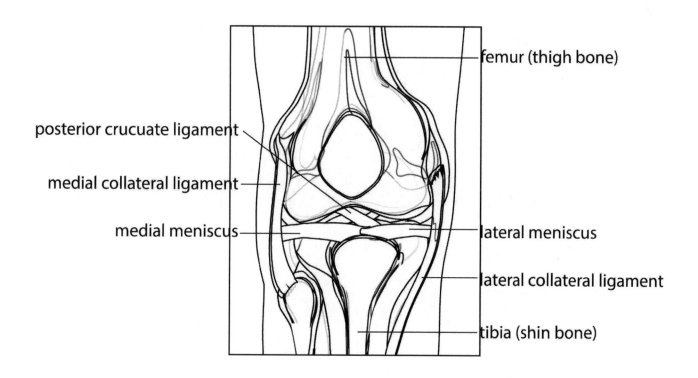

posterior crucuate ligament

medial collateral ligament

medial meniscus

femur (thigh bone)

lateral meniscus

lateral collateral ligament

tibia (shin bone)

Human Knee Anatomy

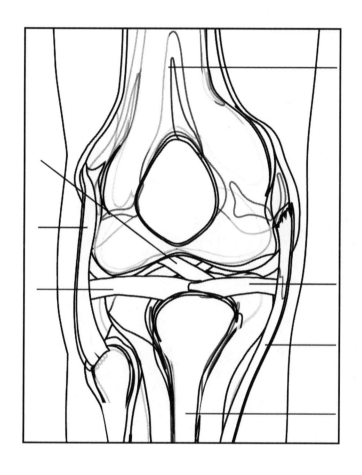

Human Knee Anatomy

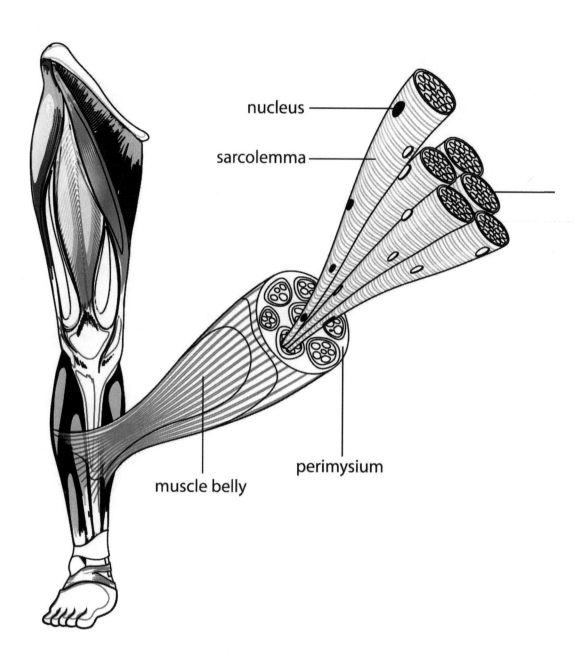

nucleus

sarcolemma

perimysium

muscle belly

Structure of Human Muscle

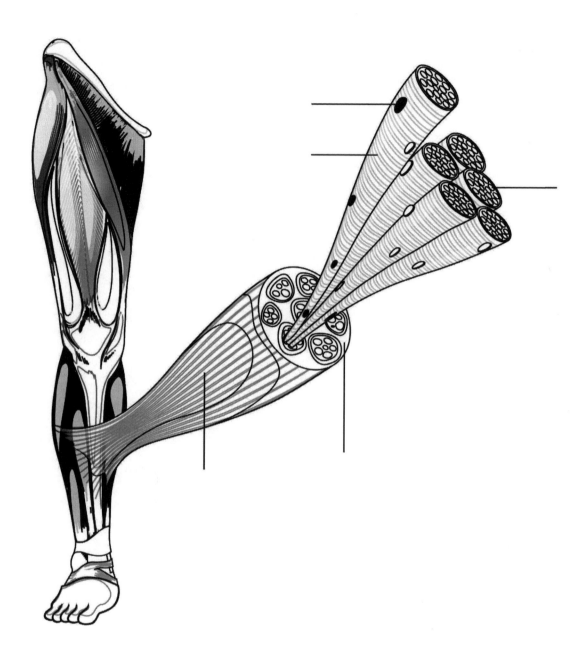

Structure of Human Muscle

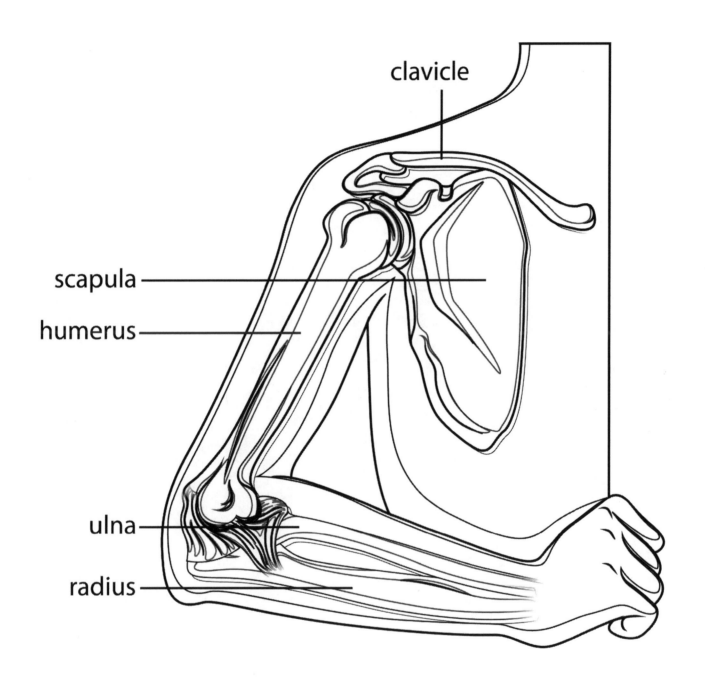

clavicle

scapula

humerus

ulna

radius

Bones of the Arm and Shoulder

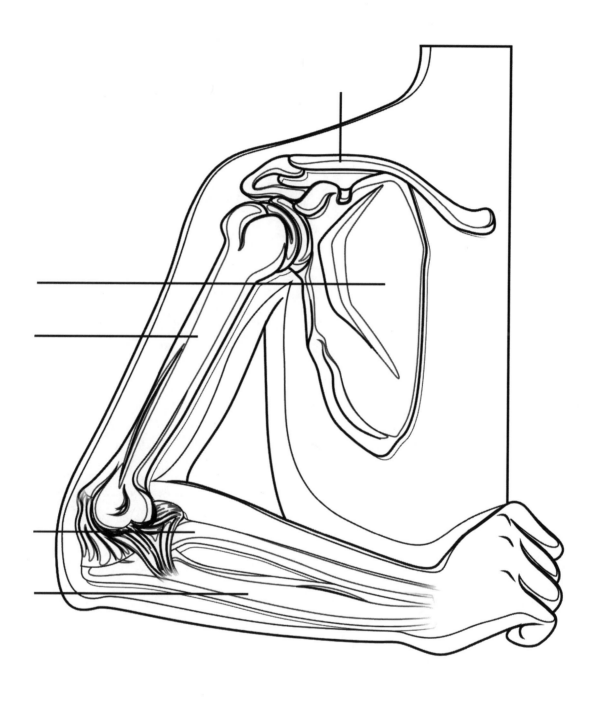

Bones of the Arm and Shoulder

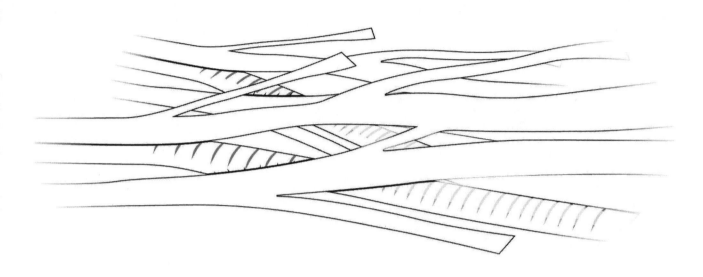

MUSCLE

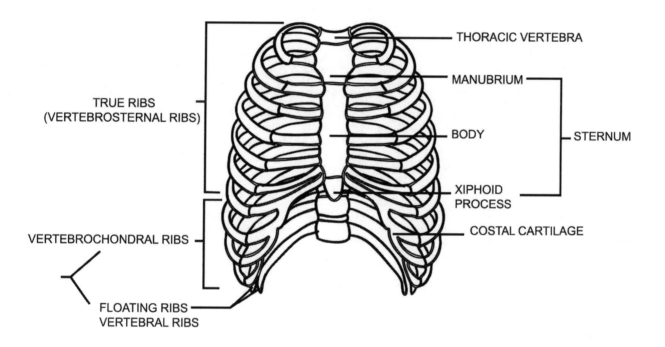

TRUE RIBS
(VERTEBROSTERNAL RIBS)

THORACIC VERTEBRA

MANUBRIUM

BODY

STERNUM

XIPHOID
PROCESS

COSTAL CARTILAGE

VERTEBROCHONDRAL RIBS

FLOATING RIBS
VERTEBRAL RIBS

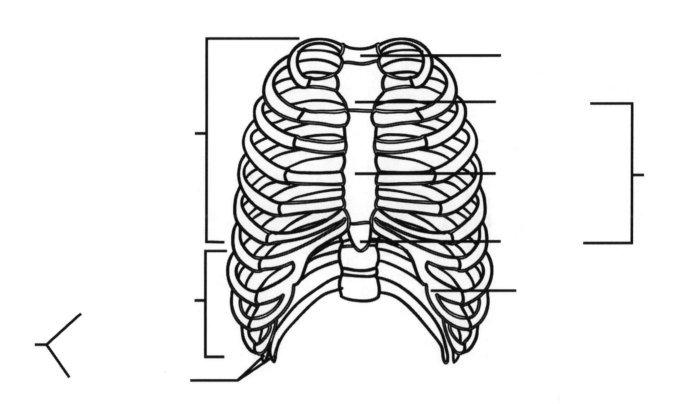

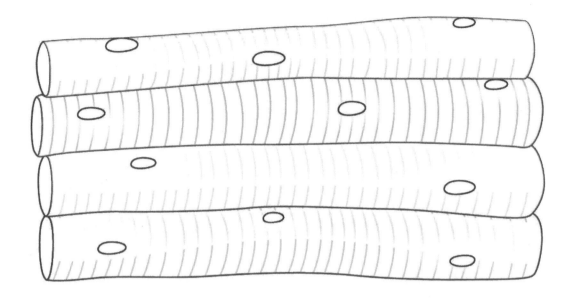

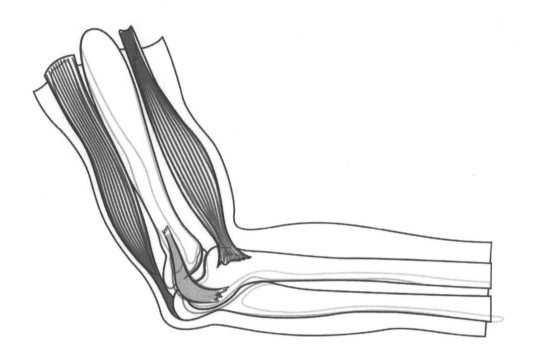

skeletal muscle

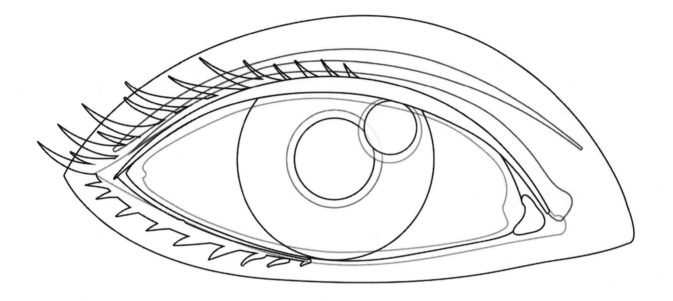

Eye

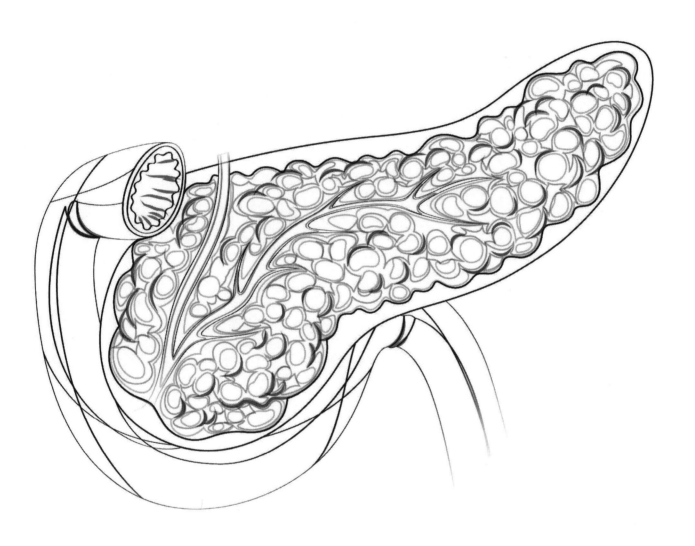

PANCREAS

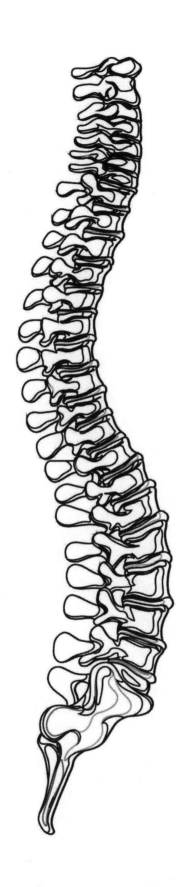

SPINE

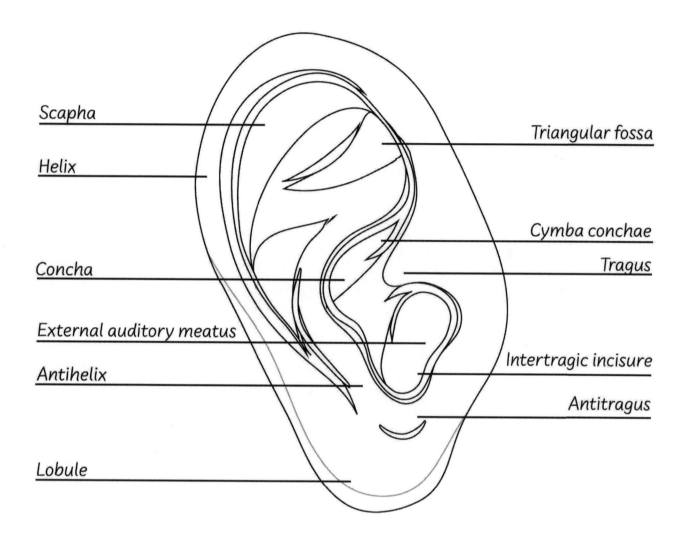

Scapha

Helix

Concha

External auditory meatus

Antihelix

Lobule

Triangular fossa

Cymba conchae

Tragus

Intertragic incisure

Antitragus

Ear

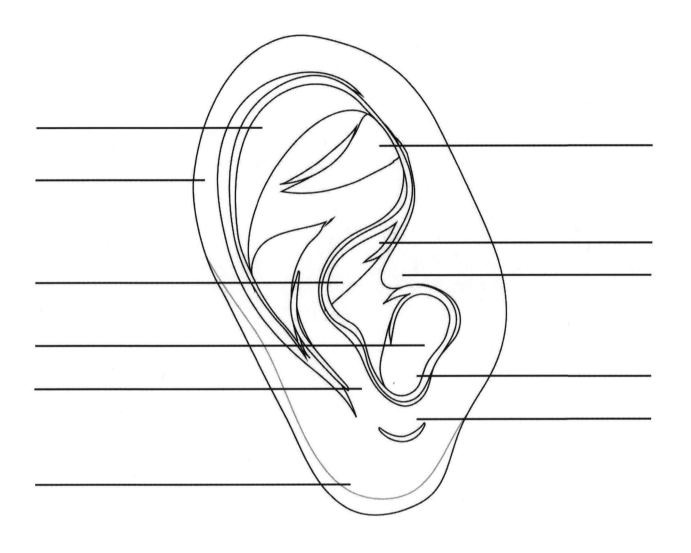

Ear

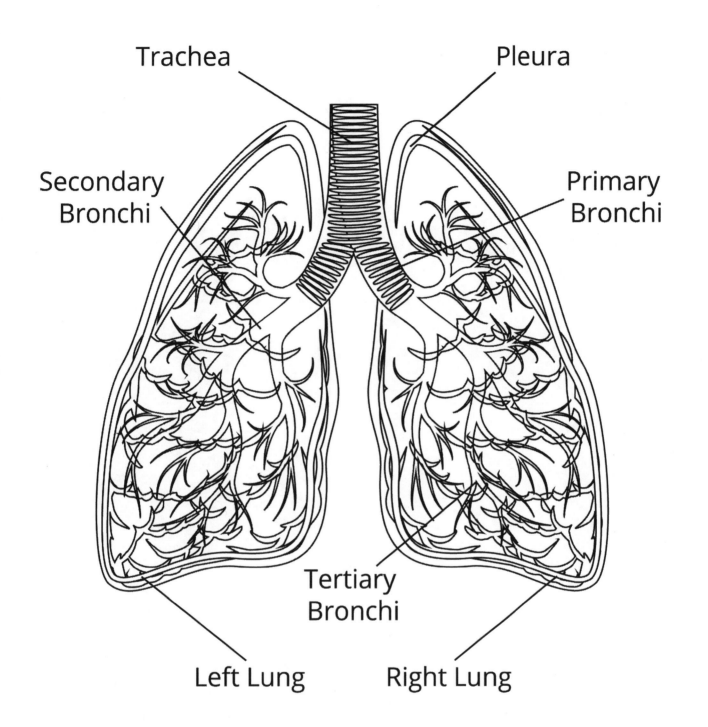

Trachea

Pleura

Secondary
Bronchi

Primary
Bronchi

Tertiary
Bronchi

Left Lung

Right Lung

Lungs

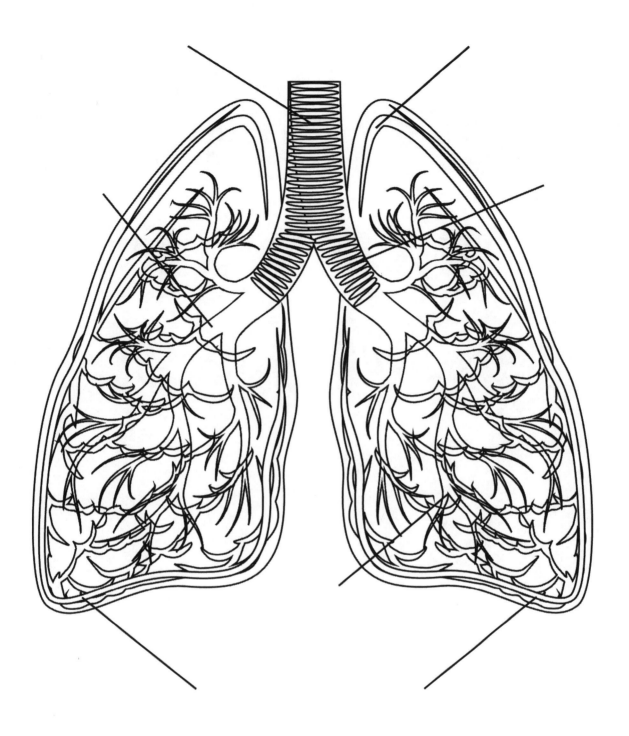

Lungs

Made in the USA
Middletown, DE
03 October 2024